Collins

Primary Social Studies for Antigua and Barbuda

STUDENT'S BOOK
GRADE 3

Anthea S Thomas

William Collins' dream of knowledge for all began with the publication of his first book in 1819.
A self-educated mill worker, he not only enriched millions of lives, but also founded a flourishing publishing house. Today, staying true to this spirit, Collins books are packed with inspiration, innovation and practical expertise. They place you at the centre of a world of possibility and give you exactly what you need to explore it.

Collins. Freedom to teach.

Published by Collins
An imprint of HarperCollins*Publishers*
The News Building
1 London Bridge Street
London SE1 9GF

HarperCollins*Publishers*
Macken House, 39/40 Mayor Street Upper,
Dublin 1, D01 C9W8, Ireland

Browse the complete Collins catalogue at
www.collins.co.uk

© HarperCollins*Publishers* Limited 2019
Maps © Collins Bartholomew Limited 2019, unless otherwise stated

10 9 8 7 6 5

ISBN 978-0-00-832491-9

British Library Cataloguing-in-Publication Data
A catalogue record for this publication is available from the British Library.

Author: Anthea S. Thomas
Commissioning editor: Elaine Higgleton
Development editor: Bruce Nicholson
In-house editors: Caroline Green, Alexandra Wells, Holly Woolnough
Copy editor: Sue Chapple
Proof reader: Jan Schubert
Cover designers: Kevin Robbins and Gordon MacGilp
Cover image: Wectors/Shutterstock
Typesetter: QBS
Illustrators: QBS and Ann Paganuzzi
Production controller: Sarah Burke
Printed and Bound in the UK using 100% Renewable Electricity at CPI Group (UK) Ltd

Acknowledgements

The publishers wish to thank the following for permission to reproduce photographs. Every effort has been made to trace copyright holders and to obtain their permission for the use of copyright materials. The publishers will gladly receive any information enabling them to rectify any error or omission at the first opportunity.
(t = top, c = centre, b = bottom, l = left, r = right)

p10 Luis Santos/Shutterstock; p11 Robertharding/Alamy Stock Photo; p12t Fominayaphoto/Shutterstock; p12b Gorlsko/Shutterstock; p13 Angela Rohde/Shutterstock; p14 Alfotokunst/Shutterstock; p15 Sean Pavone/Shutterstock; p16 PlusONE/Shutterstock; p17 Sarah Cheriton-Jones/Shutterstock; p18 IndustryAndTravel/Shutterstock; p19 Ralph Eshelman/Shutterstock; p21l ImageBROKER/Alamy Stock Photo; p21r Marina Movschowitz/Alamy Stock Photo; p22t Diana Cochran Johnson/Shutterstock; p22b ImageBROKER/Alamy Stock Photo; p23l Pascal Lagesse/Shutterstock; p23r Marekuliasz/Shutterstock; p24t COLOA Studio/Shutterstock; p24b EQRoy/Shutterstock; p25 Eric Baker/Shutterstock; p26 Evenfh/Shutterstock; p27 Diego Cervo/Shutterstock; p28 Rodney Legall/Alamy Stock Photo; p31 Malkhaz Svanidze/Shutterstock; p32 Michaeljung/Shutterstock; p33 Horon/Shutterstock; p37 Multiverse/Shutterstock; p38t Piyaset/Shutterstock; p38b GenadijsZ/Shutterstock; p39t Austinding/Shutterstock; p39b Byelikova Oksana/Shutterstock; p40 Ziablik/Shutterstock; p41t Drew McArthur/Shutterstock, p41b Kakteen/Shutterstock; p42 NOPPHARAT STUDIO 969/Shutterstock; p43 Jehsomwang/Shutterstock; p44 Modisketch/Shutterstock; p45 JJSINA/Shutterstock; p46 Hobbit/Shutterstock; p49 Luchino/Shutterstock; p50l Everett Historical/Shutterstock; p50r Everett Historical/Shutterstock; p51 Maisei Raman/Shutterstock; p52t Ellagrin/Shutterstock; p52b Rawpixel.com/Shutterstock; p53 Dnaveh/Shutterstock; p54 Sarel/Shutterstock; p55 EQRoy/Shutterstock; p56 Smile Fight/Shutterstock; p57 Es sarawuth/Shutterstock; p58 Yanik88/Shutterstock; p59t Small smiles/Shutterstock; p59b Yuratosno3/Shutterstock; p61 Kc_film/Shutterstock; p62 Andamansky/Shutterstock; p65t Red ivory/Shutterstock; p65b Pavel L Photo and Video/Shutterstock; p66 Leonard Zhukovsky/Shutterstock; p68l Ash Tproductions/Shutterstock; p68r ESB Professional/Shutterstock; p70 3DDock/Shutterstock; p71t woaiss/Shutterstock; p71b Ilja Generalov/Shutterstock; p72 Travel mania/Shutterstock.

Contents

Unit 1   Reading maps   4
About Antigua and
Barbuda   4
Antigua and Barbuda and
the Caribbean region   5
Points on a compass   6
The parishes in Antigua   7
Using a legend on a map   8
Physical features in
Antigua and Barbuda   10
Historical sites in
Antigua and Barbuda   15

Unit 2   Our cultural heritage   20
What is culture?   20
Earliest inhabitants of
Antigua   21
Other settlers   25
Ethnic groups and
nationalities   27
Local traditions and
customs   28
Local dialect   29
Importance of preserving
our culture   29

Unit 3   Government and leaders   30
What is a leader?   30
What makes a good
leader?   31
Responsibilities of
leaders   31
How are leaders
chosen?   33
What is a government?   33

Unit 4   The natural environment   34
Types of map   34
The natural landscape   36
Natural disasters   37
Man-made disasters   40
How can we protect
the environment better?   43
Organisations   44

Unit 5   Our communities   46
Population   46
Factors affecting
population density   47
Settlements   47
Population distribution   48
Communication   49
Transportation   54

Unit 6   Natural resources   58
Natural resources   58
Renewable resources   60
Non-renewable resources   60
Endangered animals in
Antigua and Barbuda   61
Conservation   62

Unit 7   Industries   64
What is 'industry'?   64
Types of industry   64
Industries in Antigua and
Barbuda   67
Links between industries   67
Workers in an industry   68

Unit 8   Trade   69
What is trade?   69
Why countries need
to trade   70
Supply and demand   71
Communication and
transportation   72

1 Reading maps

We are learning to:

- understand what an island is
- locate Antigua and Barbuda in relation to the rest of the Caribbean, and the world
- name the parishes in Antigua
- name physical features in Antigua and Barbuda
- name historical sites in Antigua and Barbuda
- name the points on a compass
- find and understand the legend on a map
- understand what the Equator is.

About Antigua and Barbuda

Our island is called Antigua and Barbuda. An island is a piece of land completely surrounded by water. Although Antigua and Barbuda are about 30 miles apart, they are considered as one state.

Where is Antigua and Barbuda?

The country of Antigua and Barbuda is in the region known as the Caribbean. You can see on this map where the Caribbean region is in relation to the rest of the world.

On a map or a globe, you will see lines running across and up and down. These lines are not real, but are used to help us locate places.

The Equator is the line that runs right round the centre of the Earth, from east to west. It divides Earth into two hemispheres, the Northern Hemisphere and the Southern Hemisphere. Antigua is in the Northern Hemisphere, along with the rest of the Caribbean region.

Antigua and Barbuda and the Caribbean region

On this map, you can see the Caribbean region in more detail.

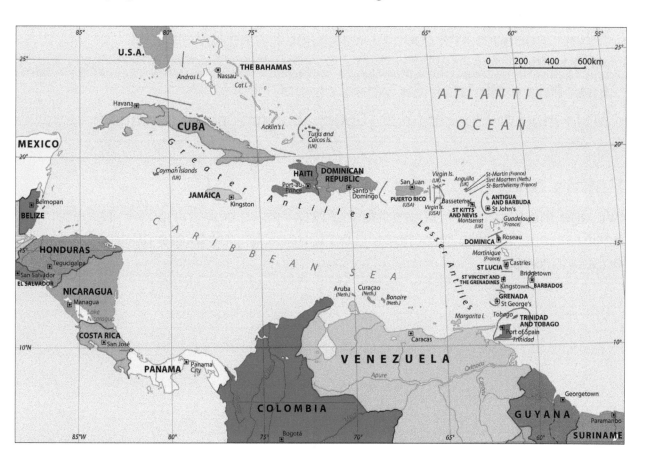

The chain of islands that make up the Caribbean region is surrounded by the Caribbean Sea to the west and south, and the Atlantic Ocean to the east and north. The Caribbean region is north of South America, south of North America and east of Central America.

Antigua and Barbuda is on the east side of the Caribbean Sea, north of Guadeloupe and southeast of Anguilla.

Facts about Antigua and Barbuda

Size: Antigua – 108 square miles (14 miles long, 11 miles wide); Barbuda – 62 square miles

Population: Antigua – 85 000; Barbuda – 1600

Independence: The country was ruled by the British until independence in 1981.

First Prime Minister: Sir Vere Cornwall Bird

Main industry: sugar (until 1960s); tourism; fishing (Barbuda)

Points on a compass

We use the points on a compass to say where one thing is in relation to another, and to give directions. The four main points are north, south, east and west.

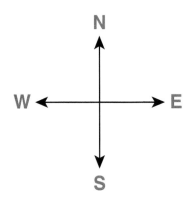

The parishes in Antigua

Antigua is divided into six parishes. You can see the parishes marked on this map. They are St. John, St. Mary, St. Paul, St. Philip, St. Peter and St. George.

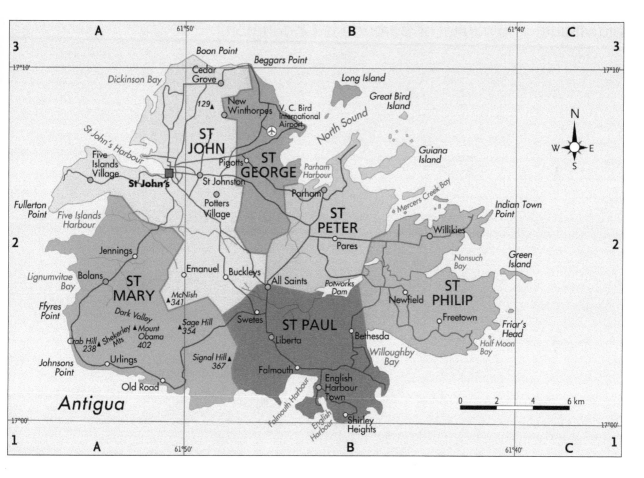

Antigua is organised into parishes to make the country easier to manage. Each parish is further broken down into towns and smaller villages.

Parish	Villages/Towns
St. John	Cedar Grove, Five Islands Village
St. George	New Winthorpes
St. Paul	English Harbour, Falmouth, Liberta
St. Mary	Bolans, Urlings, Old Road
St. Philip	Newfield
St. Peter	Pares

The capital of Antigua is St. John's, which is in the parish of St. John. In St. John's we can find many important buildings such as the hospital, banks, supermarkets, schools, post office and the police station. Many people work in the capital.

Barbuda is a smaller island and does not have parishes. It is seen as one big village. The capital of Barbuda is Codrington.

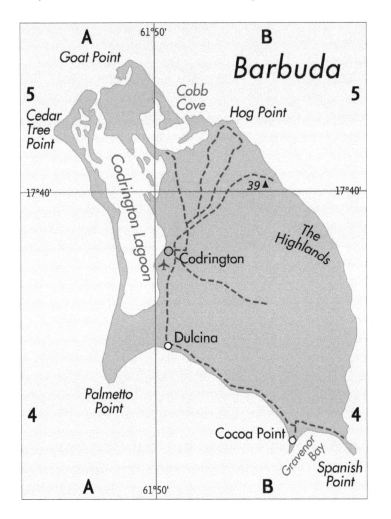

Using a legend on a map

Maps use symbols. Most maps have a legend or a key. This is what tells us what the symbols on the map mean. For example, dots on the map represent cities and important towns. A plane in a circle represents an airport.

You can see some symbols and the key on this map of Antigua.

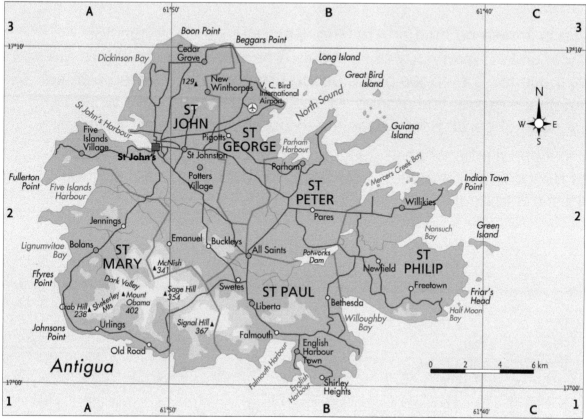

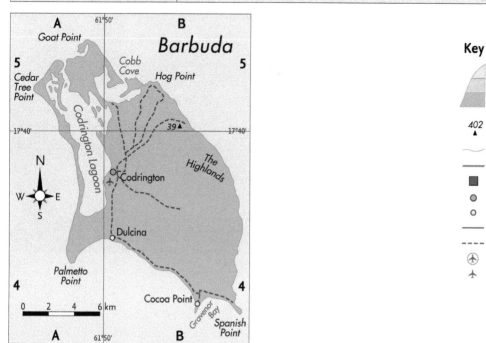

Key

	over 200 m
	100 – 200 m
	0 – 100 m
402 ▲	Mountain height (in metres)
〜	River
——	Parish boundary
■	Capital town
◉	Important town
○	Other town
——	Main road
- - - -	Track
✈	Main airport
✦	Other airport

Physical features in Antigua and Barbuda

Beaches

Antigua is known as the Land of Sun, Sea and Sand – it has 365 beaches, one for every day of the year. A beach is a place where the sea meets the land. The edges of the beach are normally covered with sand, or sometimes gravel and stones. Many of the beaches have white sand that is made of coral. Some beaches in Barbuda have pink sand.

The most popular beaches in Antigua include Long Bay, Pigeon Point, Ffryes Beach and Fort James. Low Bay and River Beach are popular beaches in Barbuda.

Long Bay, on the east coast of Antigua, is very popular with families.

High points

Antigua and Barbuda is very flat and does not have many high areas. The highest point in Antigua is Mount Obama, named after the first black president of the United States. The lowest point is at sea level. Mount Obama rises to 1309 feet (402 metres). The highest part of Barbuda is known as the Highlands but is only a little over 100 feet (30 metres) high. Other high points in Antigua include McNish Mountains, Shekerley Mountains, Signal Hill and Green Castle Hill just south of St. John's.

Mangrove swamps

Mangrove swamps are very wet areas along the coast where special trees called mangroves grow. Mangroves are plants that can live in salty water.

Swamps provide a home for plants and animals such as birds, fish, mussels and crabs. Examples of mangrove swamps include Christian Cove and Fitches Creek Swamp. You can also find mangroves around McKinnon's Salt Pond.

Frigate birds resting on mangrove at the Frigate Bird Sanctuary, Barbuda

Lagoons

A lagoon is a stretch of salt water separated from the sea by a low sandbank or coral reef. There are no lagoons on Antigua, but the Codrington Lagoon on Barbuda is home to many types of fish and birds. The Bird Sanctuary where we can see the frigatebird is also there.

Caves

A cave is a natural underground hole. There are caves in Antigua but the most well-known ones are in Barbuda.

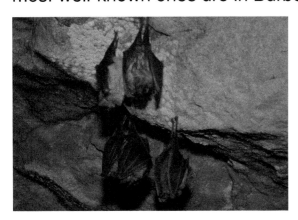

- **Bat Cave** in Antigua is home to thousands of bats hanging from very high ceilings.
- **Darby Cave** in Barbuda has a huge sink hole that is over 300 feet (91 metres) wide and about 70 feet (21 metres) deep. Palm trees grow in it.

Streams, reservoirs and ponds

There are no rivers in Antigua and Barbuda, but Antigua does have three streams. These are Ayers Creek, Cooks Creek and Fitches Creek. There are no streams in Barbuda.

Potworks Dam is not a natural feature but was built about 50 years ago to collect rainwater for Antigua. It is the largest reservoir in Antigua. Another reservoir is Wallings Dam in the south of the island.

A pond is a small area of still water. It can be formed naturally or can be made artificially. There are several ponds in Antigua. The McKinnon's Salt Pond is the largest. Others include Paige Pond just outside St. John's.

Rainforests

Parts of Antigua are covered by rainforest, especially in the higher areas. A lot of different trees grow in these tropical forests and many species of animal live there. The best-known rainforest is at Fig Tree Drive.

A helicopter view of forests in Antigua

Harbours

A harbour is a sheltered place where ships and boats can stay safely. We use the word port to mean the same as harbour. There are five main harbours in Antigua. These are:

- St. John's Harbour
- Parham Harbour
- Jolly Harbour
- English Harbour
- Falmouth Harbour

English Harbour is a good example of a natural harbour, where the water is protected by physical features. Antigua has many natural harbours.

Historical sites in Antigua and Barbuda

Historical sites are places of interest that attract tourists. They are very important as they help to build tourism, which is the main industry of Antigua. Historical sites make tourists want to come and visit our country.

Here are some of the historical sites.

Shirley Heights

Shirley Heights is in the very south of Antigua. It was a fort built by the British to defend Antigua. Some parts of the old fort are still there.

Shirley Heights

Today, Shirley Heights is very popular with tourists because it has wonderful views over English Harbour and Falmouth Harbour. There is a restaurant and bar – and a party every Sunday which both locals and tourists enjoy.

Nelson's Dockyard

Nelson's Dockyard, near Falmouth

Nelson's Dockyard is part of Antigua's largest National Park. It is in the area known as English Harbour. The British Navy used the Harbour to protect their ships and started to build the Dockyard in the 1740s, using slaves from the sugar plantations.

Nelson's Dockyard is named after Admiral Lord Nelson. It was closed in 1889 when the British Navy left and it fell into decay. It was later restored and in 2016 was declared a World Heritage Site by UNESCO.

Devil's Bridge

Devil's Bridge

Devil's Bridge is in the northeast of Antigua and is a natural rock arch. The sea is often very rough there and it has gradually worn away the rocks to form the arch.

Devil's Bridge got its name because slaves from the sugar plantations would throw themselves into the sea to escape from their slave masters.

Pillars of Hercules

The Pillars of Hercules is a natural rock formation that guards the entrance to Freeman's Bay and English Harbour. The pillars were carved by wind, rain and the waves of the sea.

The Pillars of Hercules

Fort Barrington

Fort Barrington is in the west of Antigua, on top of a hill. It was built to guard St. John's Harbour. It is the only fort in Antigua where fighting actually took place.

Fort Barrington

The Montpelier Sugar Factory

The Montpelier Sugar Factory, in the east of Antigua, was thought to be one of the finest sugar factories in the Caribbean. It was used for over 60 years before it closed in 1954. Today you can still see some of the old steam engines that were used.

2 Our cultural heritage

We are learning to:

- define the terms: 'ancestors', 'traditions', 'customs', 'culture', 'family', 'ethnic'
- name the earliest inhabitants of Antigua: the Arawaks, the Caribs
- name later settlers who came to Antigua: Europeans, Africans, Indians, Chinese
- know about some different groups and nationalities who settled in Antigua
- describe some local traditions, customs and festivals
- know about the local dialect
- know why it is important to preserve our culture.

What is culture?

When we talk about culture, we are talking about the way we live. Culture is the way of life of a group of people. Our culture includes the way we speak, dance, dress and cook our food, the music we play, the stories we tell and our religion.

The culture we have today was learned from our ancestors who came to live on our island before us. Different groups of people came to settle in Antigua at different times. Each group brought with them their own cultural traditions, which they continued in their new life. For example, our national dish, fungee and pepperpot, was brought to Antigua by the Amerindians. The dialect we speak and our dance came from the Africans, while the language we speak, as well as our major religions, came from the Europeans.

Earliest inhabitants of Antigua

The earliest known people to come and live in Antigua were the Amerindians. They came by canoe from South America looking for food. Areas of Antigua and Barbuda where they settled include:

- Twenty Hill in Parham
- Jolly Beach
- Indian Creek
- Mill Reef
- Mamora Bay
- Green Castle Hill

There were two main groups of Amerindians, the Arawaks and the Caribs.

The Arawaks

The Arawaks, also called Tainos, were gentle and peaceful people who lived in groups of families. They shared their belongings and food with each other.

They built houses made of mud, sticks and grass. The houses were round with thatched roofs.

Here, you can see an Arawak family today, and what typical houses would have looked like

The Arawaks were very clever at making things so that their life was easier. They used the natural resources around them. They made pottery from clay, hammocks from cotton, baskets from grass and beautifully carved trays from wood.

An original Arawak canoe

From stones and shells they made axes and jewelry, from tree trunks they made canoes and wooden spears. They made woven fish traps and shellfish tools to hunt animals and catch fish.

Some typical woven baskets, bags and mats

While the men went fishing and hunting, the women grew crops, such as cassava and sweet potatoes. They made cassareep from cassava juice and used it, with peppers and meat or fish, to make pepperpot.

The Arawaks worshipped the spirits of nature and of their ancestors.

The Caribs

Gradually, Antigua was taken over by the Caribs, who also came from South America. They were a fierce and warlike people and the Arawaks were no match for them. Like the Arawaks, they lived in groups of families, but the men and older boys lived in one house, while the women, girls and younger boys lived separately.

They used natural resources to make useful things like hammocks, clay pots and wooden stools. They were also good at making weapons, because they loved to fight.

A Carib stone axe and pottery

Like the Arawaks, the Carib women grew crops like cassava, yams, sweet potatoes and peppers, while the men hunted and fished.

A basket of cassava

The Carib people also had a priest whose job was to heal the sick with bush medicines. The Caribs believed in good and evil spirits. They believed that evil spirits caused sickness and death, while the good spirits brought rain and helped their crops to grow.

This is the Museum of Antigua and Barbuda, where you can see items that were made and used by the Amerindians.

Other settlers

The Europeans

After the Amerindians, other groups of people settled in Antigua. First came the Europeans.

Christopher Columbus was the first to arrive, in 1492. He travelled from Spain and when he returned there, he told others about the beautiful islands he had found. The Spanish came to the islands looking for gold and silver.

After the Spanish came the British, French and Dutch. Some came to buy and sell things, while others brought with them crops such as sugar and tobacco to plant on the island. They set up large sugar plantations and forced the Amerindians to work hard for them. Many of the Amerindians died from hard work and from the diseases that the Europeans had brought with them.

One of the first areas that the Europeans settled in was English Harbour. They were able to use Shirley Heights as a look-out point to see when their enemies were coming. They used their guns and cannons to fight off the enemies. They were protecting their ships and the island.

English Harbour and Falmouth Harbour, as seen from Shirley Heights

Betty's Hope was the first large sugar plantation. These two windmills, which were used to extract the juice, can still be seen. One of them is now a museum.

The Africans

As the number of Amerindians became fewer and fewer, the Europeans needed people to work on their plantations. They travelled to West Africa and took Africans as slaves. They were brought back to the island in the 18th and 19th centuries to work on the sugar plantations.

The Africans were treated very badly and forced to work hard without any pay. They were beaten by their slave masters and were not allowed to leave the plantation. They were often sold to other plantation owners.

Slavery was abolished on 1 August 1834. We celebrate this on the first Monday of August each year, on Emancipation Day.

The Indians and Chinese

After the end of slavery, the Europeans still needed people to work on their plantations. This time they went to India and China to find people. The Indians and Chinese worked very hard, but were paid very little. Some stayed on the island and bought shops while others later returned home.

Ethnic groups and nationalities

We often say that there are many different ethnic groups living in Antigua. An ethnic group is a group of people who are from the same race or culture – and who may share the same language. They may be Antiguan (because they were born here) or they may have another nationality. We say that they are of the same ethnicity.

Some of the nationalities living in Antigua include Chinese, Syrians, Lebanese, Indians, Trinidadians, Saint Lucians, Barbadians, Guyanese, Jamaicans and Dominicans. Each of these groups has a different culture, so we can say that Antigua is multi-cultural.

Being tolerant

Being tolerant means understanding that people are different and do things in different ways. Every culture is unique in some ways and we need to celebrate our differences. Some of the main differences in culture are in language, religion, music and food.

Local traditions and customs

Many countries in the Caribbean share the same history as Antigua – settled by Amerindians, then Europeans, Africans, Indians and Chinese – but each ethnic group has its own customs and traditions. A custom is an accepted way of behaving or doing something. A tradition is a custom that has been handed down from one generation to the next, for a long time.

Some customs we have include celebrating birthdays, anniversaries, Valentine's Day and religious holidays like Christmas and Easter. We also celebrate our National Independence. When people die, we have funerals and when people get married, we have weddings. New babies are often taken to church to be christened or dedicated.

Local festivals

As part of our local customs, we also have annual festivals. The two most popular festivals in Antigua are Carnival and Sailing Week.

Carnival lasts for 11 days, starting in late July. It always ends on the first Tuesday of August. It started as a way to celebrate our freedom from slavery. Many people from around the world come to watch or take part in it. The carnival on Barbuda is called Caribana and is held during the Whit Weekend.

Sailing Week is usually in April. Yachts and other sailing boats come from all over the world to take part in competitions.

Carnival is an event where people from different cultural backgrounds come together to have fun.

Local dialect

Our dialect is our native language/tongue and comes from our African ancestors. Dialect is often spoken and rarely written, which is why we can understand when someone speaks it, but can hardly write or read it. It is part of our local tradition.

Some common examples of dialect speech are:

- "cum yah"
- "nam um"
- "si dun dey"
- "put um back"
- "me head ah hat me"
- "na nack me"

Other customs we have include the games we play, like marbles and Warri, and using old herbal remedies when we are ill.

Importance of preserving our culture

It is very important to preserve our culture. If we don't, we can lose our cultural identity.

Families are very important in preserving our culture. A family is a group of people who live together. Each generation can pass on our cultural history to the next generation.

Grandparents talking to children and telling stories are a great way to pass on culture. Books are very useful too, as they can always be read. And schools can make sure that children learn about their cultural history.

3 Government and leaders

We are learning to:
- understand the terms 'leader' and 'government'
- explain the importance of having leaders
- outline what makes a good leader
- name the responsibilities of different leaders
- outline how leaders are chosen
- explain what a government is.

What is a leader?

A leader is someone who guides and directs a group of people. For example, the leader of your class is the teacher and the leader of your school is the principal.

The importance of leaders

Leaders are very important as they help to make sure that there is order within groups. They also make sure that the members of the group work well together to achieve their aim.

Think about how confusing it might be if there were no leaders. Imagine going to a church with no leader. How would the people know what hymn to sing? Who would give the sermon?

What would your classroom be like if there was no leader in charge?

All around us we have leaders. The pastor is the leader of the church. Our parents are leaders in the home. Sports clubs have leaders, the choir has a leader, the Boys Scouts, Girl Guides, and Boys' and Girls' Brigade all have leaders.

We also have leaders of the country.

What makes a good leader?

A good leader needs to be able to get the best out of people. They need to earn respect and to lead by example. They also need to:

- be honest
- be confident
- be able to inspire other people
- be able to communicate well (get their message across)
- be able to make good decisions.

Responsibilities of leaders

Leaders have responsibilities (things that they must do). The responsibilities depend on who they are leading and what their job is.

Country

In Antigua and Barbuda, the government is responsible for running the country. This means they decide how the country's money should be spent, for example, on roads and schools.

Gaston Browne is the leader of the government of Antigua and Barbuda (in 2019). He is the Prime Minister.

School

In a school the leader is the principal. They are responsible for running the school so that the children are safe and are learning what they need to learn.

The teacher is leader of their class and is responsible for teaching the children.

Home

At home, the parents, and sometimes the grandparents, are leaders. They are responsible for providing things such as food, shelter and clothes.

Football team

On a football team, the captain is the leader and is responsible for the team on the football field.

Can you think of other examples of leaders?

How are leaders chosen?

Some leaders are chosen because they are popular in the group. Some are given the job of being leader. Others, like members of the government, are elected by the people in a vote.

What is a government?

A government is a group of people who have the power and authority to make rules to run the country.

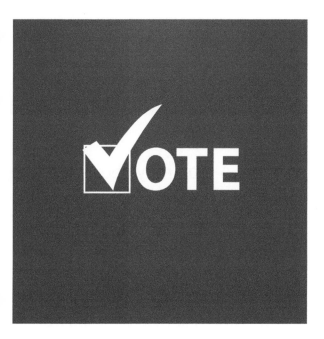

Elections

In Antigua and Barbuda, the government is chosen by an election. That is when people vote for the person they choose to represent them. When the voting is finished, the votes are counted and the candidate with the most votes wins the election.

The political party with the most winning candidates forms the government. The leader of the winning party becomes the Prime Minister.

4 The natural environment

We are learning to:
- understand the terms 'natural landscape', 'natural disasters' and 'man-made disasters'
- know about different types of maps: physical and climate
- explain how the natural landscape affects the weather
- describe some natural disasters which affect the Caribbean: hurricanes, earthquakes, volcanic eruptions, drought
- describe some man-made disasters: global warming, deforestation, dredging
- name some organisations that look after the environment.

Types of maps

We use maps to find information about a place. A map may show us the shape of the land, the patterns of weather, where people live, and where each parish begins and ends.

Physical map

A physical map is also called a relief map and shows the physical features (or landforms) of a place or a country, like hills, valleys, plains, plateaus, forests, dams and rivers. For example, a physical map of Antigua shows the shape of the coastline and how high the land is in different parts of the island. This is the natural landscape.

The physical features are usually shown in different colours. Areas of water (rivers, lakes and seas) are shown in blue and the height of different places is shown using greens and oranges. So, areas at sea level are in dark green and as the height increases the colour changes to lighter green and then eventually orange.

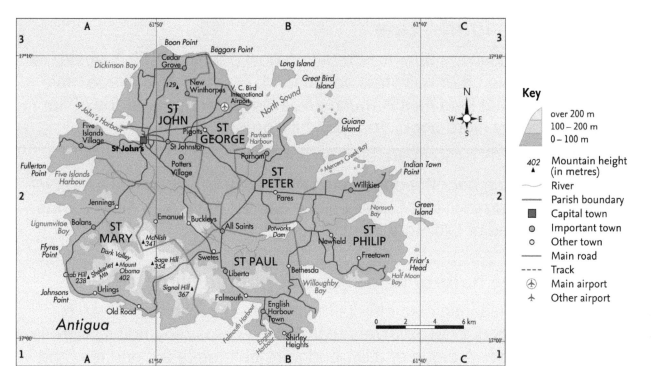

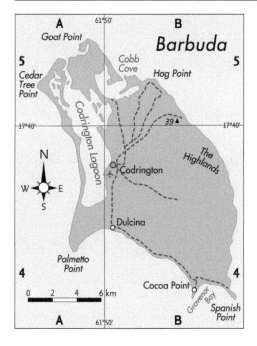

Climate map

A map can also show information about climate. For example, it shows areas that have more rain or that have dry weather. It uses colour to show areas with a different climate.

The natural landscape

The natural landscape affects where and how people live. It is easier to build homes and other buildings on flat land. Farmers also like to have their farms on flat land as it is much easier to grow crops. Areas of flat land are usually more populated than hilly areas.

Why do you think airports are built on flat land?

The people living near the coast often make use of the sea by becoming fishermen to earn a living. Fishing in the sea off Antigua is mainly done from the villages of Old Road, Urlings and Parham.

How does the natural landscape affect the climate?

The natural landscape also affects the climate of a country. When a country has lots of trees and very high land such as mountains, there is often a lot of rain. Antigua and Barbuda are both quite flat and don't have many trees, so the rainfall is low.

Changes to the landscape

The natural landscape is changing all the time. This often happens very slowly. Some changes happen very quickly, sometimes caused by the weather. Natural disasters such as hurricanes, floods and droughts, as well as volcanic eruptions and earthquakes, can change the shape of the land in an instant.

Natural disasters

Hurricanes

A hurricane is a storm with very violent winds. In the Caribbean, hurricanes are the most common natural disaster caused by the weather. They can bring down houses and trees and the heavy rains can cause mudslides and wash away soil (erosion). Hurricane season starts in June and finishes at the end of November each year.

In 2017, Hurricane Irma caused a great deal of damage in the Caribbean.

Droughts and floods

If there is no rain for a long time, a country can run very short of water. Trees and animals may die, and water has to be brought in so that people can drink. Droughts can also cause the earth to become cracked.

A really bad drought can have a major effect on the land.

If too much rain falls in a short time, during a bad storm, the land can become flooded. Very heavy rain can also cause landslides which will affect the shape of the land.

This is Havana, in Cuba. Storms caused giant waves which flooded the city.

Earthquakes

An earthquake is a sudden violent shaking, deep underground. Earthquakes can cause the land to crack. A strong earthquake can cause buildings to collapse.

Volcanic eruptions

A volcano is a mountain or hill which has a crater, or opening, in the top. If the volcano erupts, melted rock (lava) can burst through it and run down the volcano.

There are volcanoes in the Caribbean, mostly in the east, on the islands of the Lesser Antilles.

This volcano is in Indonesia.

Natural disasters affect many countries around the world, including our Caribbean islands. We can't stop them happening, but we can work to protect ourselves from some of the effects. For example, we can build homes to stay as strong as possible in a hurricane or earthquake.

Man-made disasters

Some disasters are not natural but are man-made. They happen because of the actions of humans. If we don't take better care of the environment, the damage we cause to the world may be permanent.

Man-made disasters include fires, pollution (dirtying the environment), loss of forests and loss of coral reefs.

Global warming

The temperatures in the world are rising, slowly but surely. This is what we mean by global warming. It is caused by the greenhouse effect, which you can see in the diagram. Gases that we produce collect high above the Earth and trap heat.

The gases come mainly from burning coal and also from cars and lorries.

The greenhouse effect

As well as bringing higher temperatures, global warming causes more extreme weather – so, more floods, hurricanes, droughts, and so on. These events are lasting longer and are more severe, too.

Hurricane Irma was one of the worst hurricanes ever recorded in the Caribbean. It destroyed most of Barbuda in 2017.

Deforestation

Deforestation is another man-made problem. It is the word used for clearing away large areas of forest, usually to build roads, homes and hotels.

One of the main areas where deforestation is happening is in South America.

Trees are a habitat (home) for many animals and even other plants. When the trees are cut down, the animals lose their habitat. Also, the soil can easily be washed away. This is called **soil erosion**.

To lessen the effects of deforestation, trees should be planted back to replace the ones that were destroyed. In addition, some land areas should be marked as reserved, so that the trees can't be cut down.

Dredging

Dredging means removing a lot of sand and mud from the bottom of the sea, or other area of water. St. John's Harbour is currently being dredged so that bigger ships can come in. That sounds like a good idea but it can cause pollution and change the way that animals and fish can feed.

A dredger

How can we protect the environment better?

This diagram shows some things we can do to help. We can:

- cut down pollution from factories
- use cars less
- stop cutting down trees, or replace them by planting new ones
- recycle more
- use less plastic.

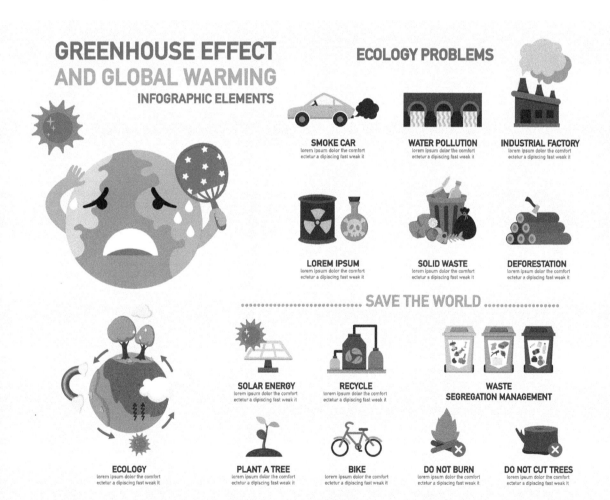

GREENHOUSE EFFECT AND GLOBAL WARMING
INFOGRAPHIC ELEMENTS

ECOLOGY PROBLEMS

SMOKE CAR
lorem ipsum dolor the comfort ectetur a dipiscing fast weak it

WATER POLLUTION
lorem ipsum dolor the comfort ectetur a dipiscing fast weak it

INDUSTRIAL FACTORY
lorem ipsum dolor the comfort ectetur a dipiscing fast weak it

LOREM IPSUM
lorem ipsum dolor the comfort ectetur a dipiscing fast weak it

SOLID WASTE
lorem ipsum dolor the comfort ectetur a dipiscing fast weak it

DEFORESTATION
lorem ipsum dolor the comfort ectetur a dipiscing fast weak it

SAVE THE WORLD

SOLAR ENERGY
lorem ipsum dolor the comfort ectetur a dipiscing fast weak it

RECYCLE
lorem ipsum dolor the comfort ectetur a dipiscing fast weak it

WASTE SEGREGATION MANAGEMENT

ECOLOGY
lorem ipsum dolor the comfort ectetur a dipiscing fast weak it

PLANT A TREE
lorem ipsum dolor the comfort ectetur a dipiscing fast weak it

BIKE
lorem ipsum dolor the comfort ectetur a dipiscing fast weak it

DO NOT BURN
lorem ipsum dolor the comfort ectetur a dipiscing fast weak it

DO NOT CUT TREES
lorem ipsum dolor the comfort ectetur a dipiscing fast weak it

Organisations

There are some organisations in Antigua and Barbuda whose job it is to take care of the environment.

National Office of Disaster Service (NODS)

This is a local organisation which helps us to know what to do if a disaster is going to happen. For example, they go into schools to teach us what we should do if there is an earthquake. This is the drill:

HOW TO SAVE YOURSELF DURING AN EARTHQUAKE

①

DROP
DOWN ONTO
YOUR HAND AND KNEES

②

cover
YOUR HEAD AND NECK

③

HOLD ON
TO YOUR SHELTER

The Environmental Awareness Group (EAG)

This is a team of volunteers whose main aim is to protect our natural environment. They teach us about how important it is to look after the environment and give us tips about how to do it, for example, by saving water.

The National Solid Waste Management Authority

This organisation works to help keep the environment clean in Antigua and Barbuda. It collects waste from our homes, schools, hospitals, markets and other places, and recycles it as much as possible. Anything that can't be recycled is taken to the Cooks Sanitary Landfill to be disposed of safely.

5 Our communities

We are learning to:

- define the terms 'population', 'population density', 'settlement'
- say the factors that affect population density
- explain how settlements develop
- describe the population distribution in Antigua and Barbuda
- explain how communication and transportation have developed in Antigua and Barbuda, and name some changes that may occur in the future
- describe cities, towns and villages.

Population

The population of Antigua and Barbuda is the total number of people living on the islands at a particular time. Every 10 years, the number of people is counted in what is called a census.

There are people living all over Antigua, but some areas have more people living in them than others. This is known as **population density**. Areas around the city of St. John's are densely populated, while areas around the coast are sparsely populated.

Factors affecting population density

Why do more people choose to live in or near St. John's? There are several reasons:

- Public transport is better.
- The land is flat, which makes it easier to build homes.
- There is not a lot of forest land.
- The soil is good for growing food.
- There are lots of job opportunities in St. John's.

Settlements

A settlement is a place where people live. A group of people will live in one of the following:

- a village
- a town
- a city.

The first people who came to live in Antigua, the Amerindians, settled mostly around the coast, where they could catch fish. Some then moved inland where they could farm, as long as they could get to the coast easily.

Gradually, as transport and communication improved, people moved to other parts of the island. They looked for places that had a good supply of clean water, that had high ground (to see any enemies more easily), and where there were natural resources they could use.

Population distribution

This map shows the population density today, in the different parishes in Antigua and Barbuda.

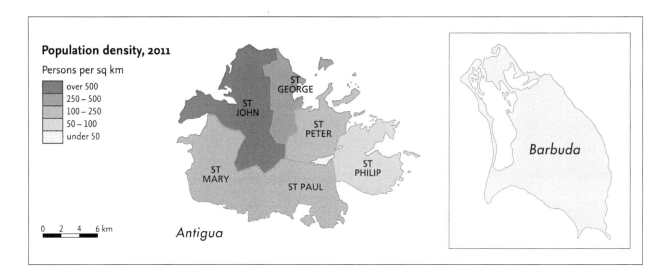

Population density, 2011

Persons per sq km

- over 500
- 250 – 500
- 100 – 250
- 50 – 100
- under 50

0   2   4   6 km

Antigua

Barbuda

The parish of **St. John** and the surrounding areas are densely populated. This is where the capital of Antigua is and where there are important buildings such as the hospital, post office, shops, banks and schools. Many people also work there, so choose to live nearby.

The parish of **St. Peter** is less densely populated. This is because there are areas of industry and a lot of land that is used for farming.

The parish of **St. George** is also not well populated. There are many factories as well as the airport, and these occupy huge amounts of land space.

The parish of **St. Mary** has a lot of forested area as well as farmland which means that a lot of people do not live in those areas.

The parish of **St. Philip** is the least densely populated on the island.

Communication

Communication is the sending and receiving of messages. There are various ways to do this and it has changed a lot in the last 50 years.

Communication then

Communication in the past was very slow. People used horns, bells, birds and other signals such as smoke from fire.

Then came the telegraph, which meant it was possible to send and receive messages.

A Morse code machine used to send telegrams

Letters were handwritten and mailed via the post office to persons in other countries. It might take weeks for the letter to be sent and to receive a reply!

Things improved a lot with the telephone, which was invented in 1876. For the first time it was possible to speak directly to someone in another place, although it was a long time before people could afford to have one at home.

The telephone was invented by Alexander Graham Bell.

Someone using the first telephone

Over time the telephone was used more and more. However, because it had to be connected to a cable, it was not possible to move it more than a few feet.

Telephones through the ages

Communication now

The internet

Today, messages can be sent and received instantly from anywhere in the world, using the internet. Communication is instant. At first, this was done by email with a computer, but that is now being replaced by the mobile phone.

Mobile phones

Telephones became smaller, wireless and mobile. You can take a mobile phone almost anywhere with you and still speak to someone.

And with the internet on your phone, you can now use it to send text messages and do video calling. The mobile phone is the main means of communication today.

Where next?

In the next 30 years, it is possible we will communicate by saying nothing at all! How? Just by using our thoughts...

Another possibility for the future is smart lenses. These are like contact lenses that you wear in your eyes. This will let you take pictures and record videos by just blinking your eyes.

Transportation

Transportation is the means by which people and things are moved from one place to another. There are three forms of transportation:

- Land – cars, buses, vans, bicycle, donkeys
- Sea – boats, ships
- Air – airplanes, helicopters

Land transportation is used to move people and things around Antigua, while sea and air transport have to be used to get people and things to Barbuda. There are two types of transportation: public and private. Public transportation is that which can be used by everyone who pays the fare. Private transportation is owned by families for their own personal use.

Transportation then

At first, the only way to travel anywhere was on foot. If you wanted to move anything, you had to carry it.

The earliest form of transportation in Antigua was the canoe, used by the Amerindians. The Europeans then used carts drawn by donkeys and horses. After the end of slavery, the local farmers depended on the donkey as their main form of transport.

Bicycles became very popular and replaced the donkey for many journeys. Steam locomotives were used to transport sugarcane.

Transportation now

Today, we have a large choice. We have cars, vans, buses, lorries and trucks that can transport people and goods across the island. We use boats and airplanes to travel to other countries as well. These types of transport allow us to get to where we are going comfortably and quickly.

The bus station in St. John's. This is public transport, for use by people who prefer not to use a private car.

Where next?

In Antigua, and in many other countries, there is a move to increase the use of electric-powered cars and reduce the use of gasoline. Electric cars are much better for the environment as they don't give out harmful gases.

Charging an electric car

Next in line will be self-driving cars, and drones to deliver goods.

There used to be a TV show called 'Meet the Jetsons', which was about a family living in the future. Their form of transportation was a flying car. Although this was shown on TV over 30 years ago, we are seeing the things they used becoming a reality now.

By the time you are adults, the car you drive will be very different from what you see today.

Flying taxi, anyone?

Drones can be used to deliver goods.

6 Natural resources

We are learning to:
- define the terms 'resources' and 'natural resources'
- name examples of natural and man-made resources
- name examples of renewable and non-renewable resources
- name animals in Antigua and Barbuda that are endangered
- explain the term 'conservation'.

Natural resources

Resources are all around us. A resource is anything that is useful. There are two main types: natural resources and man-made resources. A natural resource is anything found naturally in our environment, while man-made resources are things that are made by humans, such as plastic.

Plastic is a man-made resource.

Examples of natural resources include:

- diamonds
- sunlight
- trees
- copper
- gold
- freshwater
- silver
- animals
- soil
- air/wind
- coal
- petroleum
- natural gas
- people.

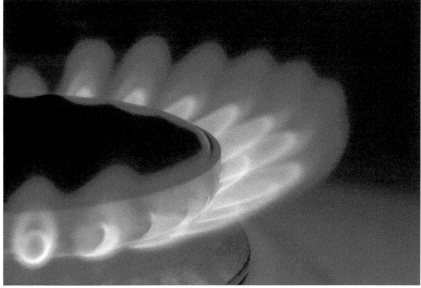

Coal and gas are natural resources.

Natural resources can be divided into two groups:

- renewable
- non-renewable.

Renewable resources

Renewable resources are things that can be replaced. We use water every day: to cook, to wash, to bathe and to drink, but the water that we use is replaced when the rain falls. We cut down trees, but new ones grow back when we plant seeds. We breathe in oxygen (air) daily, but more oxygen is produced by plants.

Examples of renewable resources include:

- fresh water
- air/wind
- sunlight
- trees
- animals.

Non-renewable resources

Non-renewable resources are the resources that we cannot make more of and that cannot replace themselves. These are mostly found in the ground.

If we use up a non-renewable resource, there will be none left. We use sand to make the cement to build our homes, and if we use it all up, we won't have any more to use. More sand can be created, but it would take millions of years.

The fuels that we burn for energy, such as oil and coal, are non-renewable. Examples of non-renewable resources include:

- coal
- copper
- natural gas
- petroleum.

Endangered animals in Antigua and Barbuda

Antigua and Barbuda is home to many species of animals. Some of them are in danger of becoming extinct, which means they will not exist anymore. They are called **endangered species**.

The destruction of their habitat (home) is one of the reasons for this. Another reason is that too many are being killed for food.

Endangered animals in Antigua include:

- racer snake
- West Indian whistling duck
- European fallow deer
- spiny lobster
- hawksbill turtle
- leatherback turtle.

An Antiguan racer snake

A leatherback turtle on its way out to sea after laying her eggs

Conservation

We need to take care of our natural resources and use them wisely. Some, like trees, can be replaced but it only works if we plant enough new ones to replace the old ones.

We need to conserve our natural resources and be sure we don't waste them. Water is a good example. We need it all the time but if there isn't enough rain, we end up having a drought. In order to conserve water, we can reuse it, for example, by using water from washing clothes to water the garden. You can see lots of ways to save water on the next page.

Water your yard and outdoor plants early or late in the day to reduce evaporation.

Use a shut-off nozzle on your hose.

Choose plants that require less water.

Mulch around plants to hold water in the soil.

Get an Energy Star labelled washing machine.

Use a low flow showerhead.

Take short showers – five minutes or less is best.

Turn off water while soaping hands and brushing teeth.

Turn off sink faucet while scrubbing dishes and pots.

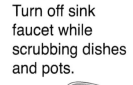

Install new toilets that use less than 1.6 gallons per flush.

Put faucet aerators on sink faucets.

Use a broom, not a hose, to clean driveways and walkways.

There are organisations which help us to protect our environment by educating us about what to do and what not to do. One such organisation is the Environmental Awareness Group (see page 45).

7 Industries

We are learning to:
- explain the term 'industry'
- name the four types of industry: primary, secondary, tertiary and quaternary
- give examples of industry in Antigua and Barbuda
- explain the link between different types of industries
- explain the role of employment.

What is 'industry'?

A fisherman catches fish and sells it. A farmer plants crops and harvests them to sell. A carpenter is paid to build homes for people. A teacher comes to school each day and helps children to learn. All of these people earn money for the work that they do.

These workers are all doing an activity. Any activity that earns money is called an industry.

Types of industry

There are four main types of industry:
- primary
- secondary
- tertiary
- quaternary.

Primary industries

In primary industries, the workers take things from the land and sea, which they then sell. Fishing, farming and mining are examples of primary industries.

Mining for different metals

Secondary industries

In secondary industries, the workers take the things from the land and the sea and make them into something useful. This is usually done in a factory. For example, cotton is picked from the plant and taken to a factory where it is made into thread, and then that thread is made into cloth which can be used to make clothes.

Here, fish is being treated and then put into tins, in a fish factory.

Here are some examples of products made in secondary industries from the raw materials in primary industries:

Raw Material	Product
Coconut	Coconut milk, coconut oil, coconut powder, sugarcake
Cotton	Thread, clothes
Wood	Paper, furniture
Fish	Tinned tuna, saltfish
Cowhide	Leather belts, shoes and bags

Tertiary industries

In tertiary industries, the workers do not produce any goods, but instead they provide a service. Teachers, nurses, lawyers, doctors, bankers, mechanics, electricians, taxi drivers and plumbers are examples of workers in tertiary industries. This type of industry has the most workers.

These police officers in St. John's are providing a service.

Quaternary industries

In quaternary industries, the workers are highly trained and usually very skilled. They may work in scientific research, consulting or information technology.

Industries in Antigua and Barbuda

In this table you can see examples of industries in the different categories in Antigua.

Category	Activities
Primary	fishing, farming, hunting, sand mining, quarrying
Secondary	agro-processing, manufacturing, cottage industries
Tertiary	transportation services, bank services, teaching, tourism, retail services, building services, arts and crafts, security services
Quaternary	computer technicians, software developers, researchers

Links between industries

All industries are linked in some way. Think about tomatoes. If there is no farming to grow tomatoes, there is no tomato ketchup made in factories and we would not be able to go to the supermarket to buy the ketchup.

Another example is making cars. That is a secondary industry, but look at how it links to other industries too.

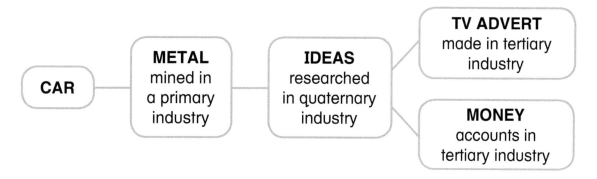

So, if we remove one of the industries, we disrupt the whole chain.

Workers in an industry

The different activities provide work for adults to do. This is called a job. When adults work, they receive money in return (a wage or salary). They use the money they earn to take care of themselves and their family by doing things such as buying food and paying bills.

Some of the money goes towards helping to develop the country. This money is called a tax. Taxes are collected by the government and the money is used to provide services for the people in the country – building roads, providing health care, and so on.

8 Trade

We are learning to:

- explain the term 'trade'
- explain why countries trade: imports and exports
- understand the terms 'supply' and 'demand'
- understand why communication and transportation are important for trade.

What is trade?

Read these two short stories.

> John is at school and looking forward to break because he's hungry. When he looks in his lunch bag, he finds the one flavour of crisps that he really doesn't like. They must have been the only ones left at home.
>
> Then he sees his friend Tom, who has the flavour that he likes!
>
> 'Hey, Tom, can we swap?' asks John hopefully.
>
> Tom agrees and they exchange crisps. Everyone is happy!

> Jane wants to cook some soup. She checks what she needs and finds she doesn't have any sweet potatoes. She rushes off to the market and gets there just in time to buy some.

These are both examples of trade. The only real difference is that in the first story there is no money involved. John swaps crisps with his friend. Jane buys her sweet potatoes with money.

In the past, before we used money, people exchanged goods so that everyone had what they wanted. If you caught six fish, you could exchange some of them for the vegetables that someone else had grown. This is called **bartering**. Now, we nearly always use money to trade goods. If we want bread, we go to the baker's and pay for some.

Trade is the buying and selling of goods and services. We trade with other people all the time. We buy clothes, shoes, food, books and medicine. We go to the doctor and the dentist. We build houses and buy furniture to put in them.

Why countries need to trade

Many of the things that we buy are not made in Antigua. They are made in other countries. That is because we do not have the raw materials that are needed to produce those goods. Antigua and Barbuda imports most of the goods that the people use. These include vehicles, electronic items and other household items like ovens and refrigerators.

Just as a person trades with another to get what they need, so countries trade with each other to get the goods and services that their people need, and to get raw materials. It is more complicated, especially when the countries trading use different currencies (types of money) – but the principle is the same. In Antigua we use the Eastern Caribbean (EC) dollar, but the US dollar will often be used for trading.

Import

When a country buys goods and services from another country, it is called importing. For example, Antigua and Barbuda buys flour from St. Vincent and the Grenadines, so we can say Antigua imports the flour.

Export

When a country sells goods and services from another country, it is called exporting. For example, when St. Vincent and the Grenadines sell flour to Antigua and Barbuda, we can say St. Vincent exports the flour.

Supply and demand

Supply is the number of goods that are produced for sale. **Demand** is the number of goods that people want to buy.

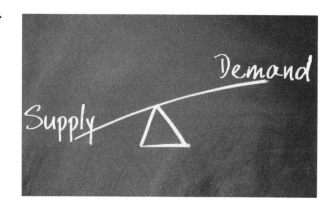

When there are more goods available than the country needs, we say that we have a **surplus**. The price of the goods then tends to go down so that people buy more of it.

On the other hand, if people want to buy more of the goods than are available, the price of the goods tends to go up and fewer people want to buy them.

Here is an example.

Sam grows coffee in Jamaica. One year, a hurricane damaged a lot of his crops. He and the other growers couldn't produce many coffee beans. The price went up, and so people stopped asking to buy the coffee as they couldn't afford it. Sam and the other growers planted new coffee plants and a few years later they had a really good harvest. There was a surplus of coffee beans and the price went down. Coffee became very popular again.

This is how supply and demand work.

Communication and transportation

Trade today has to be fast and it has to be reliable. It requires good communication and good transportation.

Transportation

Goods need to be transported. That may be within a country, when it will probably be by road or rail. If goods are going from one country to another, it may also be by ship or by airplane. Huge containers are used, which means that more goods can be moved easily across the world.

Moving goods around, from the seller to the buyer, is called **distribution**.

You can see the containers that have been taken off the ship.

Communication

Good communication is very important for trade to work well. The phone, and particularly the internet, have both made communication much faster and more reliable. Buyers and sellers can contact each other directly and instantly.

It is also possible to get real time updates as to where the order is currently located as it makes its journey to its final destination. In some countries software such as GPS can give the exact location for the delivery of goods.